The Pale Handbag of the Apocalypse

The Pale Handbag
of the Apocalypse

Poems by

Eileen Jones

IRON
PRESS

First published 2014 by IRON Press
5 Marden Terrace
Cullercoats
North Shields
NE30 4PD
tel/fax +44(0)191 2531901
ironpress@blueyonder.co.uk
www.ironpress.co.uk

ISBN 978-0-9575032-1-2
Printed by Field Print, Boldon Colliery

Typeset in Georgia
IRON Press books are distributed by Central Books
and represented by Inpress Ltd
Churchill House, 12 Mosley Street,
Newcastle upon Tyne, NE1 1DE
tel: +44(0)191 2308104
www.inpressbooks.co.uk

Supported using public funding by
ARTS COUNCIL
ENGLAND
LOTTERY FUNDED

For Andy

Eileen Jones lives in Tynedale, Northumberland and is the editor of the *IRON Book of New Humorous Verse* (IRON Press 2010) and the author of the pamphlet *Connecting Flight* (Red Squirrel Press 2013). Her poetry career began when she was fifteen with the publication of a satirical poem in *Jackie*, but was mostly put on hold until a few years ago. In the intervening decades she worked in social care and mental health as a social worker and manager.

CONTENTS

Visions of the Apocalypse

Playing games before the Apocalypse

Visions
of the
Apocalypse

The Pale Handbag of the Apocalypse

I do love a good handbag ... I think they could be either a great
divider or uniter... I'm on the uniter side. I think no one should
make fun of anyone else's handbag choices. – Hillary Clinton

The launch keys for the nuclear array
the solid sounding 'gold codes' are
written on a 'biscuit' – not that Doomsday
if it comes, will be sparked by a hard
fired Speculoos or home-style shortcake –
this biscuit is a snappy plastic card
Amex shape and size, and convenient
to slip inside the jacket of the President.

It's said that more than one head man has shocked
his staff, by misplacing the precious key card.
Rumours Reagan kept it in his sock
may have been debunked; not so, it seems
the story Carter left it in the pocket
of a suit that went for cleaning. Clinton, we
are told, did much the same – due perhaps
to some internal short-lived moral lapse.

The common factor is the perpetrators
of these gaffes, apocryphal or real, were men,
with crucial matter kept in outer layers
of their clothing. Layers they might shrug off when
keen to show their rolled-up sleeves. Greater
focus has ensured Barack remains a gem
of vigilance; his aides are maybe brighter,
the stitching of his pocket linings tighter.

But why not use a safe container: some sort
of bag? Granted, a man bag for the chief
is tough to spin, and a backpack? Who'd court
the likely flak for that one? Would the image grief
be less with a small version of the sporty
'football' case that holds the military brief
and 'gold' phone for the relay of instructions
once the snapped biscuit triggers mass destruction?

Far easier for a Presidential 'she'
to keep the biscuit safe when jacketless;
uncontroversial common sense decrees
it's hard to stow some items in a dress
and normal for a woman's office keys
to be bagged in with her personal effects.
Wielding her black Asprey was Thatcher's brand;
perhaps one reason why Frau Merkel's favoured hand

pose is her unfettered 'diamond'. But it's hard
for any woman to stay bag free; once she's back
from a photocall, Angela reclaims – not Prada
elegance – a bright and roomy sack.
The main female US aspirant is far more
pro chic handbags. Hillary applauds their knack
of bringing unity. But will a hot pink purse
suit her minders? They'll surely be averse

to standout hues; in mushroom tones less risk it
will be sighted. Not trusting it to Bill, she'll lean
close on it when it contains the biscuit;
at state dinners she might borrow from our Queen
a hook with suction cup in which one spits
to stick it to the table. This handbag will mean
business though; let no one think it safe to make their moves
on something primed with sulphur, flames,
                                    the thundering of hooves.

The Last Judgement

Alma Mater

If things go badly at the end
I'll find eternal lodging
on a wooden bench, mouthing grace
in an old school-dining-hall
low ceilinged and north lit
where sullen women loom
behind a rank of plastic wash-up bowls
to dole out knotted sausages
or spent spaghetti dressed with grit,
and – after I've joined a line
and made my offering to the pigs –
they'll bless me
with a tough jam square
roofed with matted coconut and hair
and sluiced with ashen custard.

Mosaic in the Cathedral of Santa Maria Assunta, Torcello

The roasting damned
have been located near the door
to hook the sight line
of the congregation leaving after mass
so that the faithful might receive
caution and lasting sustenance
from slabs of darkness;
from something sharp edged,
impossible to chew,
before they emerge
into sweet, deceiving radiance.

Larkin About

After *This Be The Verse* by Philip Larkin

Children everywhere are socialised by their peer group, not by their parents. – Stephen Pinker

They fuck you up your little mates.
They may not mean to but they do,
And if they're vicious reprobates
You'll end up anti-social too.

But they were fucked up in their turn
Before they'd even left their cots,
By tiny thugs with nought to learn,
Who beat them up at 'Tumble Tots'.

Child hands on misery to child
In every simple playground game,
So if your darlings grow up wild
It isn't you they have to blame.

The Facts of Life

At seven years old
shocked when my mother told me
about the mortgage

Audit Blues

to the tune of Wichita Lineman

I do the spying for the County
so you'd better stay right –
I'm searching through your files
for that little oversight,
but if you're feeling lucky
throw those boring forms away
I'm your County Hall nightmare
come on, make my day.

Communication

I know that I know what I know.
I don't know if you know what I know.
If you don't, then should I let you know what I know?
What if you want to know but you're not meant to know what
I know?
Or you are meant to know but you're not meant to know it
from me?
I don't know.
Do you know that I know what I know?
And if so,
Should I know what I know, do you know?
In this organisation
There's one consolation:
I know that I know what I know.

White Water on the Funding Stream

*Ring-fencing of funding streams may need to be considered ... It should
be seen as a fundamental tool to underpin the current raft of changes.*
— From NHS Confederation 'Action points'

Your team is tasked
with the construction of a current raft
from this ring-fencing.
You are asked to use
the fundamental tool supplied
and to ensure
all underpinning is secure
before the launch
upon the funding stream.
Do not employ
the fundamental tool
except to underpin.
You must ring-fence the funding stream
before the launch
but not in such a way
as to impede the progress
of your current raft.
When all is clear,
cascade instructions fully
to your team,
select your ring-fencing,
collect your fundamental tool,
put on your wetsuits, and begin.

Pebbledash

Imagine: a lowland Scottish town,
a street of hardware shops
and bakeries with greasy pies –
those deep ones
with casings that can crack unwary teeth.
Suppose this upright place decides
to twin, not with some gloomy ville
in northern France, but with Burano
the Venetian island
famous for its lace,
a tilting campanile
and the rainbow stucco of its streets.

Back home from summer junkets
where Prosecco flowed,
the Scottish worthies
view their town with different eyes,
begin to chip at pebbledash
and peel it from their bungalows.
The hardware shops restock with outdoor paint
in jade and lavender. The carry-out
while selling shoals of squid
can't shift its battered cod;
the townsfolk switch from stovies to polenta.
Old women put aside their scratchy wool
to peer at cobweb lace

until October sleet attacks
the gorgeous bungalows;
a frost clips off the blooms
exposed on granite sills;
the townsfolk look abashed and hanker for
those thermal pants they flung to charity.

The town, as if caught out in underwear
too sheer and gaudy, makes a grab
for rough grey overcoats,
and pebbledash sweeps back;
people vote to swap their twin
for 'Villemorte sur Marais'.

And yet, the bungalows still wear
their vibrant under layers.
It only needs a hotter sun
baking each gritty carapace,
to split it like a chrysalis.

Words for a cliff

In my French novel
the gloomy hero climbs a high cliff
to brood about the war.
I stop reading to listen to the news
and hear the woman say
her whole life is in her home
and she's been refused
a last admission to pick scraps
of meaning from its frame,
now that her garden's crashed
into the back yard of the house below
with every root and stem and clipped twig,
all the spade-scarred clay
shearing from a new cliff edge.

Back in the book I learn
the French hero is a soldier
grieving for a lover driven mad.
He's on the brink of *la falaise*
a word whose sound defies
its sense: with that final syllable
gliding from a smooth top ledge,
down to a lapped shore.
Our word gets closer
with its one strike beginning
like a cleaver parting meat
but it fizzles to extinguishing
so at the end is not enough,
not sharp enough.

Copiapó, Chile 2010

Words of the miners
trapped in the dark
of the President's pocket.

The Control Tower

She is flying in the dark
without altimeter or compass
and even the clock is useless.

She is flying in the dark;
all she has to steer by
are my words, blurred in her ear.

She is flying in the dark.
Alone in this control tower
with my maps and charts
I am searching a closing sky
and trying to talk her down
trying to bring her here.

Winter

From Peterborough northwards, pin-sharp air
snipes in through a window gap.
Outside there's whiteout, snow shin-deep
while in here, a technical glitch
has frozen hot drinks from the trolley.
The woman swears, buys miniature gin
and frowns at her copy of *Heat*.
Opposite, the boy's mouth tightens as he taps on Facebook,
until boredom, like a shark's fin,
breaks the surface with a sigh.
Ripples lap his mother's chin, tilting it upwards.
'Pack it in,' she snaps. 'For the last time, pack it in.'

Night Sounds

I know it's you. I hear you flap from the roof
of a thrumming train on the far side of the Tyne.
I hear you settle and scrabble on slate
before you bat-squeak in my loft.
I hear you kick the hands of my clock
or tap dance in my bath,
or kettle along the pipes in the wall,
or crack knots in the floor.
When you stop shredding the silence
it only gets worse: that's when you start
to flip, flip, flip with your beaded claws
in the space behind my ribs, beside my heart.

The New Taboos: Forthcoming Titles

*It would be good to see you tackle more taboo areas
in your writing...*

Sell that Kidney on the Net
Neutered Tigers: Better Pets?
The Healing Power of Cigarettes

Dolphin Farms: The New Small Pens
Tasty Ways to Cook GM
Tummy Tucks for Under Tens

Cosy Fur to Rear at Home
Nuke the Whale, Restore the Dome
Pit Bull Packs: Their Right to Roam

Global Warming's Lighter Side:
(Where to Surf the Rising Tide)
How to Tan your Rhino Hide
Crack Cocaine: The Pre-School Guide

Playing Games before the Apocalypse

Flat Pack Fling

This is Roger. We've just met
and are about to become intimate.
He'll go with anything, they said.
Now he's mine and I uncover
his smooth blond legs, make sure
his other parts are present and correctly
formed. Size is important here.

As I take a grip on his hard
frame, it's a question of keeping
things straight and coupling
only those parts which are meant to fit,
with a lot of fumbling exertion
and sweating into positions
unkind to crumbly knees, and cursing.
I'd hoped this might be simpler,
forgetting that he's Swedish.

I turn him over and with more
moaning and sweat we're almost there.
With one last push he's finished.
So am I. I light a cigarette
inhale deeply, sigh, and press
my bottom to his nicely padded seat.

Accessible Verse

My poems are too easy – it's a shame.
I tell them they should try to raise their game:
'Just be more circumspect – enigma's prized.
Don't come across too soon, you'll be despised.'
I'd hoped one day to see them bound in leather
but they've never learned to keep their knees together.

I've always done my best to dress them well
in Sestina, Terza Rima, Villanelle;
with obscurity, allusion – all a waste:
on them these arcane jewels look like paste.
'You need', I say, 'someone who'll take their time,
not get off on some cheap and quickie rhyme,
who'll feel their way towards your inner light,
who'll take you home and stay with you all night.'

'If we're so free and easy', they reply,
'you need to ask yourself the reason why.
Life's short, we want our fun, so don't go pressing us
on creeps who'd like to spend three hours undressing us.'
I have to let them go although it hurts
to watch them sashay off in see-through shirts.
I send them to the world and when they're gone
don't kid myself they'll keep their knickers on.

Drama Shorts for Women: the Vital Ingredients

If this is your first effort you need to know it's crucial
for females in your drama to be middle-aged and rueful
about broken veins and dreams and HRT and cellulite
and the fact that men are all completely shite.
Or make them lasses on the pull applying lippy in the bog
trying to top each other's stories of their most disgusting snog
and cracking Breezer-fuelled jokes
about the universal uselessness of blokes.
Any males should all recount amusing histories of failure
and be obsessed with football and the size of genitalia –
don't worry about depth here, their function's to impart
the writer's theme that lads are helpless farts.
The title only needs to be catchy and unique
like: *Nuns From Outer Space Stole Me Granda's Talking Leek.*
Get all your near and dear ones there to see it, they'll be chuffed
and without this last ingredient you're stuffed.

Foreign

For once, we have a balcony
above the courtyard's loud geraniums
its crackle tiles and pots,
the hum of citrus and a shock
of bright blue butterflies.
A springing cat
is foreign-featured in a style
we can't pin down.
The street-far traffic drone is spiked
with horn blasts, the whine of mopeds
and the cries of children shifted
to a different key, and through the fissures in
the slab of noise, tenor voices rise
rehearsing something that we almost recognise.

Sex, Death and Maltesers

Ode

Melting, velvet, teasing spheres
slip from your red cellophane
and yield your dusky coating
to my tender stripping teeth.
Your golden airlight sweetness
fizzes on my tongue and is
so easy to possess.

A Brownish Airball Foresees its Fate

Jostling here in the darkness,
comforted by our sameness,
clinging together like sheep dung
we are doomed to dissolution,
to be ripped from this frail sachet,
for the wash of slavering acid,
the cruel broaching teeth,
and looming here in the darkness
is the red and slimy grimness
of our approaching birth.

Party Types c.1975

For Linda France

I say I'll go along with Di –
she doesn't show – I don't know why.
I wait an hour then take a cab;
the same old crowd are in some pub
except a handful who, like me,
take invitations literally.

Virginia's here, she's lost her head
and found the Spanish lodger's bed
succumbing to his Latin chat,
she's never learned to smell a rat
and thinks they're puppies anyway.
Di's just phoned, there's some delay;
she's stopped to buy a bottle or
something else – you know the score –
which means she might show up at one
if nothing better comes along.

I look around for likely men
but as they've stayed away again,
I wander to the kitchen, where,
kind Martha with her wispy hair
and spriggy frock, her cheeks all red,
is fussing over garlic bread
while Annie, fiddling with a knife,
sobs out the story of her life.

As soon as I can get away
I take my chance. Back to the fray:
the extroverts have left the pub

are making inroads on the grub
and Hilda's here, she's looking grim
she's had another row with HIM
(it's safer not to ask her why).
Of course there's still no sign of Di.

Virginia appears – he's Greek
not Spanish – she is looking meek
but smug. She whispers in my ear,
she's found her dream at last. I fear
a week at most will puncture it.
I say as much to Hilda but
she isn't in a mood to hear.

Sophia sits and sips her beer
and smiles, she's seen it all before.
I sit beside her on the floor;
she reaches out her hand for mine
and tracing out the feathered lines
she sighs. It seems my road is long –
the heart line weak, the head line strong.

Just then the noise goes off the scale
and silence follows, then a wail
as Hilda's palm strikes Spiro's cheek.
He yells a lot of outraged Greek
but Hilda grabs Virginia's arm
and shakes her. Ginny in alarm,
flees weeping to the kitchen where
kind Martha gives her tea and care
and Annie, gleeful, starts to tell
how men have made her life a hell.

Sophia has to feed her goats;
we stumble off to find our coats
and as we're heading for the door
we hear the telephone once more.
Di's just about to catch a plane
she'd like to, but she can't explain.
She has to go, they've called her flight,
'I'll ring,' she promises, 'or write.'

Outside the night is warm and clear;
swifts flicker in the summer air.
We walk, Sophia lives nearby,
and talk and laugh and wonder why
and later as we share some wine
and tell ourselves our lives are fine,
our stories better with no hero,
the door flies back and in walks Spiro.

The Offside Rule

A table in a bar
my keys, two glasses – 'This one's Cantona'
a salt and pepper goal
and Beckham has possession
of a knot of cellophane.
The eye is quicker than the brain.
I might have grasped Cardassian ludo
or that game they played on Dr Who
in six dimensions.
He smiles – indulgent, wise and smug:
this man who has possession
of a knot of mystery.

Veggie Chant for World Cup '98

Meat-free pancake roll
Come on England give us a goal!
Tofu burger, soya mince
Come on Shearer, come on Ince!
Veggie fans are mean and hard
Tougher than a nut roulade!
We're bad, we're wild, we're off the leash
Our bellies full of spinach quiche!

Six Great North Run Haiku

– Training –

under a late sun
plodding at my side –
my shadow

jogging uphill
I'm overtaken
by forty Friesians

– The Race –

in slow queues
the women suffer
penis envy

not far past the start
six firemen in full kit
burn me off

at the seventh mile
I'm just trying to keep
gob off my trainers

I'm carried
towards the finish
by the tide

The First Principle of the Yoga class

The first principle of the yoga class
is to slap your mat
on the floor
before
some pushy bitch
nabs your pitch.

Grey Lace

A found poem for two voices, after Mills & Boon and Zanussi

First carry out a rinse and spin
His body is awesome –
without any garments
he's still a leashed beast she thinks –
The door will be locked
while the familiar animal attraction
throughout the delay time
flickers in her erogenous zones –
The delay time can be changed before
flames begin to lick the tight pink buds
initiating the start/pause button
of her breasts.

Some vibration is inevitable
A throbbing need tightens his groin
especially if mounted on a wooden floor;
as he pushes down
the hose should be reset by loosening
her wide-legged pants exposing
the ring nut and
the shadowed valleys of her body, and then
the feet should be adjusted and the drum checked
as he enters her, millimetre by millimetre

If the appliance is overloaded you will hear
she is making small sounds of pleading
an audible warning signal
as he delays the liquid fire of fusion

Remember it is necessary to wait
until ...
until the cycle has finished
until their passion crests ...
before the disconnection of the inlet hose.

In Residence

They found me a room near the plant
in a mean terrace, without central heating.
At night the gas fire stuttered
and I curled up alone with Iris,
losing myself in all that middle-class complexity.
But afternoons were best: I left off reading
to watch the towers blur and soften
in the fading February light
and, leaning on the sill, I sucked
the rank, thick power from that damp air,
turned up the volume
as Queen's great anthem played.
They're dreamlike now and distant
those Middlesbrough days.

Invocation to the Muse

If you'll spare me a moment, Lady Muse,
I'll make you an offer you won't refuse.
I can cut you in on a winning scheme,
I'm not over bright but I have a dream
of A-list glory and Costa prizes
and all the comforts that Man devises.

I ought to make it clear from the start
I'm not one of those who'll suffer for Art.
I'm not into madness, booze or despair
taking up arms or living on air.
All I want is a saleable story
to fill up this empty page before me;
it doesn't have to be deathless prose
if it pleases the punters anything goes.

Inspiring the great is a tired convention –
a noble aim, but is there a pension?
Abandon those heirs of Austen and Proust!
I can give your credit rating a boost
if you'll just supply the creative lead
and leave me to come up with the greed.

Creatures
of the
Apocalypse

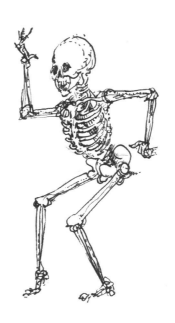

Urban Gull

No huddled gape for town gull young,
no head frills, mouth tufts, not much cute
in his beak sharp look – new sprung

egg fresh, primed, onto an office roof,
this chick is footsure, focused, pecking.
He's no easy rat-snack – don't be fooled

by his fluffy down, his brown speckled
sleepsuit – this hustler is all grab and eat
and strut, squawking – not for herring.

Menus change. His dad's heisted chips are sweet
and fast, his mother slickly fetches back
a whole ham sandwich. Swapping shore for street

was a no-bird-brainer. Their son will own this patch,
this screech of sky; his quickfire kind
have drilled our flimsy urban shell and cracked it.

Cumbrian Alpaca

They come from mountain plateaux in
Peru, these round-eyed
camel cousins

whose padded feet tread lightly
on tender ground; who copulate
sitting down and breed easily;

who defecate and urinate
in a single corner of their field,
and do not bleat, but communicate

by low humming; who only feed
moderately on native grass
and do not stampede

or bite; whose cloudy fleece is lustrous
and was formerly
reserved for high born Incas;

whose eyes are curving glass
reflecting, on this dismal day,
light from a southern pass
thousands of years away.

Black Hamster

She didn't qualify for the dog –
not even a Scottie;
it seems you have to be someone substantial
to be tailed through your gloom.
Instead, she has been allocated 'Midnight'
who twitches from his nest of straw
to pedal his nocturnal wheel,
dismounting every now and again
to peer through the bars as if checking
whether the scene has shifted
before he stuffs his cheeks with grain
and then patters,
with grim satisfaction
back to his wheel,
back to his gnawing and treading.

Peeved Fritillary

Fritillary butterfly on a giant thistle, Lindisfarne

I'm not your flutterby –
don't let me hear you nutters sigh
'elusive wondernets' etcetera –
I neck my nectar
from the spiky
It suits my style, it suits my psyche
I'm hard – I came from hard, turned into a case
after I'd looped my gut and stuffed my face,
and got outta my skin a few times.

Most of my kin
got the one way trip to a shouty nest –
I took a spin
then hung around in a gulletproof vest
until I cracked it – one of the few –
got my wings, got my strip:
black checks on rust –
think girders, think sponsored by Irn Bru;
don't print me on your girlie pants
don't ink me on your curdled flanks
don't post me on your profile
or your cutesy birthday card
– not me – I'm hard.

On this tidal island's brutal coast
watch me ride rodeo,
straddling a bucking bloom
in storm force 'vroom'
watch me neck my giant thistle shots off
suck them up then get my rocks off
so that I
can lay my eggs and die.
I'm not your flutterby.

Jellyfish Stranded

On the fork-rippled fringe
of this panhandle of land
your frilled skirts
are snarled in sea wrack
and dogfish purses.

Before you lost your way,
let go your urge to clench and pulse,
your glory was your gloss,
your star whorls and webbed striations;
you glowed like amber or the moon.

Remembering the salt surge,
did you yearn for waves to float you,
long for a tide too slow to turn?

Eclipse

Sun
shadowed
by the Moon
attracts our gaze
and makes us restless. Cattle calmly graze.

Rescue

The envelope was damp and charred
and taped in polythene. An official card
declared fire damage to the contents,
in case this wasn't clear.
I steer towards the rational
when probing the mysterious,
so resisted dark suspicion of a vandal's
application of a cigarette or spark.
The scorched remnants of the letter
expressed the warmest sentiments,
a likely indication of spontaneous ignition –

but I never leap towards the obvious.
After further thought I realised
a lost and newly landed
immigrant from Venus had misidentified
(and this makes sense) a metal cylinder,
red and brimming with combustibles,
as a handy outdoor heater in this chill
and coastal region of our planet.
She must have introduced her long
and incandescent digit via the slot
and the subsequent wailing of the sirens
will have scared her into hiding.

Now there's a sea fret on the way
and it's down to me to rescue her.
Her intentions aren't malign;
her companions may be scattered
or even splattered
and not everyone can make
my calm appraisal of these matters.

Rats

'You're never more than ten yards from a rat,'
she says. I look in all directions,
try to gauge the distance
and listen for scuttling
or squeaks, thinking:
they might be nearer.
I have to have a plan.
A roomy isolation bubble
would be the surest way
to guarantee
my whole ten yards immunity.
But rodents are resourceful:
one day some crafty specimen
might ride in on my lunch tray.
No. Better take my chance outside,
be braver, choose a single rat
fiercer than most,
have it groomed
and trained to scamper
in a wide circle around my feet
to keep the rest of them at bay.
A rodent minder or a spirit guide:
who knows?
We might get ... close.
It might appreciate my jokes –
they say rats have a sense of fun
and like to play.
If so, right now I'd guess
they're laughing at us.
From thirty feet away
or maybe even less.

Extract from 'One Hundred Ways to Hide'

The Hare: flattening – recommended
for those who might have lost their boxing skill
The Hedgehog: sphere-ing – not recommended
not even for the spiky and the still
The Chameleon: tinting – recommended
only for the moody and the slick
The Wildebeest: herd-centring – recommended
only for the pushy and the quick.

The Leopard: dappling – recommended
for the stealthy and those who like to spring
The Rabbit: freezing – not recommended
for anybunny, not for anything
The Peacock: dazzling – recommended
for those who need to get right in our faces
The Cockroach: crevice-ing – only recommended
for the lovers of the dark, the hardest cases.

After the Apocalypse

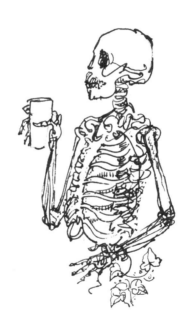

Anniversary on Another Planet

At breakfast I felt his gaze, steady as ever
resting lightly on my third shoulder –
I sometimes think my shell has grown paler there.
We hardly spoke. I watched his foot fondly,
twelve digits trapped the tumbling bread
in that deft way he has. Of course, he always
finds it hard to voice his feelings –
his endearments are as rare as jungle rain.
But last year he remembered even though
the larva harvest failed in spring; the grubs
were late pupating and each wizened chrysalis
would barely feed our seventeen newborn.
It's evening now and fire snails are spawning
I fear their winter hatchlings might fledge early.

Belgium

When he moved in she found herself in Belgium.
He stacked her fridge with urine-tinted beer
and gummy-shouldered jars of mayonnaise.
As she inhaled the briny stink of mussels
and the stench of fat, her borders seemed to shrink
encompassing only what was flat and vegetal.
His voice grew guttural, and full of phlegm
his greasy jeans as overstuffed
as breeches on a Bruegel oaf.

She threw him out, but chose to stay in Belgium.
Most afternoons she polished dark veneer,
spread her linen tray cloths
edged in lace, filled porcelain bowls
with light-whipped truffles. The rippling chimes
of carillons lulled her. She dreamed
she lay behind stepped gables,
that she gazed for hours at oyster shells
or dewdrops on the perfect skin of apples.

Flying to the Blue-domed City

October was grey and raw
and quiet strangers lifted you
and set the dark between us.

Two seasons later,
high above the snow-bright mountains
in a Russian plane,
I scanned the peaks for wreckage
and monitored the engine's drone

until the sunlight burned my fear
to dreams of a green island,
with its silver veins feeding the mulberries.
The blue-domed city,
tiled with stars and spun by worms
for Tamerlane, was mine.
You might have found
a different city, another Samarkand.

One Woman's Small Resistance

For Jeri

Being clever, hard working, not given to rows
had left a conspicuous mark on her brow;
with her boss taking aim at the slightest cue
she'd almost bitten her tongue in two
and her in-tray swelled like something alive
until crunch time loomed one Thursday at five
with a target missed, an appraisal due
her job on the line, what could she do?

That night as she tidied her underwear drawer
seeking distraction in this homely chore
she remembered hearing that risqué knickers
bloom under the cassocks of some lady vicars.
(A natural urge whose outward expression
may be somewhat fettered by their profession
is given free rein in this harmless way.)
She pondered anew on her showdown next day
then chose the best terms for her rage and despair
and embroidered them all on her roomiest pair
of briefs in some detail. (Anything skimpy or racy
would have called for prodigious efforts in précis.)

Next day, there was no getting out of meeting
her rude appraiser. But on taking her seat in
his gloomy lair, she felt silky text against her skin
and his sarcastic gibes seemed unusually thin.
As he droned on she mused: You obnoxious lout, you!
If only you knew what my keks say about you!
A thought that somehow gave her the strength
to refute his false slurs with calm and at length.

There was no looking back. The rat had no teeth
for someone with shiny armour beneath
her quiet demeanour. Inspired to cut loose
she set up a small concern to produce
her ground-breaking range of control
undergarments. Soon she was in a whole
new ball game: record funds from 'Dragons Den'
bankrolled her pitch to beleaguered men
(virile and punchy printed retorts
on 'Y-me Fronts' and 'Boxed-in Shorts').

So take heart if you feel that this miserable age
of recession compels you to sit on your rage;
you might be less prone to intemperate rants
if the perfect riposte is inscribed on your pants.

Empty Sky

After the eruption of the Eyjafjallajökull volcano in April, 2010

No chalk scribbles on the smooth blue
wash, no orange tailfins coated
in unseen dust, no engine roar – no risk
of something trollied, pink and cabin-size
dropping on our town.
And no one queued, clutching shoes
and explosive toothpaste rendered safe
in slide-seal sandwich bags.

Near-to-Heathrow dwellers
were only buzzed
by Highland ospreys heading home
and no-fly days were crowned by no-fly nights
when, looking up, we knew
what streaked across a thumbnail clip of moon
must be a meteor, a satellite
or something more mysterious.

The crush
of grounded dreams
and ruined blueberries,
was nowhere near the worst of it,
but still ...

Tarzan's Lament

First stanza by Sean O'Brien, from his Guardian online poetry workshop exercise. Included with the poet's permission.

Give me a pear from the blue bowl, Jane.
Give me five a day, for old time's sake.
Peel me a grape, disembowel a fig.
Let fruit be waiting when I wake

from fitful sleep and nocturnal pain,
to morning's even grimmer ache:
knowing I'm cast as the next big
tabloid fool – proclaimed as a fake

by the pictures of my pad in Bahrain
and the private jet I used to make
the jungle trips. The high-tech safety rig
we swung on blithely over the lake

was finished by craftsmen. Vain
now seems the trouble they'd take
to camouflage with leaf and twig
each nylon line. My heart will break

remembering how you'd furnish, Jane
our canopy kitchen with pans you'd take
from your scholar pa. You stole for the pig
who grunted over your soft traybakes

so coarsely, who only aped the swain
and ought to perish in your lake
of tears. Feed the fruit to the chimp! Then dig
a pit for me, your own vile snake.

Take Me To Your Ready Room

Jean-Luc Picard, please let it be my fate
to count the stars reflected in your pate.
It's no surprise I've fallen hard for you;
you're in a different quadrant from your crew.

Will Riker, brave, but not as sharp as most,
is not your thinking woman's piece of toast.
While Geordi's mind is crisply analytical,
there's no way he could get my warp core critical.
Nor could Data, though his bits are all correct
and he has by far the biggest intellect.
And Worf? I couldn't snuggle up in bed
to someone with a corrugated head.

As for the women, anyone can see
they yearn for you, Jean-Luc, and just like me,
they hear that wistful timbre in your voice.
But look around you. Have you got a choice?

That stuck-up medic, Crusher? Surely not.
Who spawns a kid like Wesley should be shot.
Don't even think of making Troi your squeeze.
An interstellar social worker? Please!
And Guinan? Leave her to her Vulcan gin
and Klingon cocktails. You're not taken in
by seers in silly hats; you're too perceptive.
Besides, her name sounds like a contraceptive.

Mon Capitaine tout seul! It's me you seek:
your cup of Earl Grey tea, I'm hot and weak.
We're meant to be, Jean-Luc, it's futile to resist
you might escape the Borg, mon cher, but I'll persist.
Oh beam me to your side! You have to know
I'm yours, Jean-Luc, if you'll just make it so.

Mariana in the Moated Grange Gets a Life

after Alfred, Lord Tennyson

But comes the day she lifts the latch
The scales new fallen from her eyes
She hires a bloke to mend the thatch
And dredge the moat and kill the flies
She gets a grip, she goes to law
And has the Grange put in her name
She's no one's footstool any more
She grabs the day and stakes her claim:
'I'm through with that absent rat, no fear he'll
blag his way into my bed
so he needn't bother to show up here
unless it's to fix the sheds ...'

1989–

For Andy

They packed their old Trabants at last
and took the Wall apart for souvenirs.
In German class,
I only got as far as *entschuldigung*
and *tschüss*. But there was a dismantling
for me as well, nudged by your Christmas postcards
from Jaipur and Kathmandu, and a new
assembling, with nothing missing from our sky
on the day Mandela walked, unbroken,
the day he stepped out of the songs and posters,
out of the streets that wear his name.
Even now I hear his voice with your music,
none of it swallowed by the dark;
one of us will gather up the keepsakes –
all our pictures always come apart.

Notes

The Hillary Clinton quotes on page 11 are from an interview in the March 2011 issue of Harper's Bazaar: *Hillary Clinton, Myth and Reality.*

In *In Residence,* the literary residency at a chemical works in Middlesbrough is imagined.

Peeved Fritillary was inspired by an encounter on Lindisfarne with a dark green fritillary butterfly. They are especially powerful fliers and are the only fritillaries found in Orkney and in the Outer Hebrides.

The online poetry workshop devised by Sean O'Brien, which inspired *Tarzan's Lament,* appeared on The Guardian website in March 2008 www.theguardian.com/books/2008/mar/10/poetry. *Tarzan's Lament* wasn't submitted to the workshop.

Acknowledgements

Larkin About was first published in *The Guardian Weekend Magazine* (letters page) in response to an article by Stephen Pinker.

The New Taboos was first published in the Zebra Press anthology, *The Book of Ten.*

The Control Tower and *Winter* were previously published in the pamphlet, *Connecting Flight,* Red Squirrel Press, 2013. *Winter* was Poem of the Month on the Diamond Twig website, February 2013.

Flat Pack Fling was first published in *The North.*

The Offside Rule was first published in *Red Herring,* the Northern Poetry Library's magazine.

Belgium was published in the Literature Northwest online anthology, *The Hat You Wear.*

Flying to the Blue-domed City and *In Residence* were published in a Diamond Twig postcard series.

Take Me To Your Ready Room was published in the IRON Press anthology, *Star Trek the Poems.*

Thank you

To Peter Mortimer for making the book happen, to Kate Jones, Andy Waterworth, Joe Waterworth, Andrew and Becky Jones, Lesley Dellow, Alison Malcolm, Sandra Marsden, Elaine Whipp, Sheila Wakefield, Ellen Phethean, Sue Rylance and all the members of Carte Blanche writing group and the Lit & Phil Tuesday poetry group for their encouragement, inspiration and support; to Andy Croft for his invaluable instruction in ottava rima at a Carte Blanche session; to Sean O'Brien for kindly allowing the use of the lines from his workshop exercise; to Jo Reed for her inspired illustrations, and to Anna Woodford, the owner of the original (non-nuclear) pale handbag.